Sports Illustrated KIDS

HOCKEY'S GREATEST
MYTHS AND LEGENDS

by Elliott Smith

CAPSTONE PRESS
a capstone imprint

Published by Capstone Press, an imprint of Capstone
1710 Roe Crest Drive, North Mankato, Minnesota 56003
capstonepub.com

Library of Congress Cataloging-in-Publication Data
Names: Smith, Elliott, 1976- author.
Title: Hockey's greatest myths and legends / by Elliott Smith.
Description: North Mankato, Minnesota : Capstone Press, [2023] | Series: Sports illustrated kids: sports greatest myths and legends | Includes bibliographical references and index. | Audience: Ages 9-11 | Audience: Grades 4-6
Summary: "Did the U.S. men's Olympic hockey team really win the gold medal by beating the Soviet Union in 1980? Do Detroit Red Wings fans really throw octopuses onto the ice at home games? Do hockey players really get to take the Stanley Cup home with them? Get ready to learn the real stories behind these and other great hockey myths and legends!"—Provided by publisher.
Identifiers: LCCN 2022025129 (print) | LCCN 2022025130 (ebook) | ISBN 9781669003632 (hardcover) | ISBN 9781669040316 (paperback) | ISBN 9781669003595 (pdf) | ISBN 9781669003618 (kindle edition)
Subjects: LCSH: Hockey—Miscellanea—Juvenile literature. | Hockey—History—Juvenile literature. | Legends—Juvenile literature.
Classification: LCC GV847.25 .S546 2023 (print) | LCC GV847.25 (ebook) | DDC 796.356—dc23/eng/20220427
LC record available at https://lccn.loc.gov/2022025129
LC ebook record available at https://lccn.loc.gov/2022025130

Editorial Credits
Aaron Sautter, editor; Bobbie Nuytten, designer; Donna Metcalf, media researcher; Whitney Schaefer, production specialist

Image Credits
Associated Press: Art Everett, 11, Mary Altaffer, cover (left), Tampa Bay Times/Dirk Shadd, 9, The Canadian Press/Jason Franson, 8; Getty Images: Bruce Bennett Studios, 28, Jonathan Daniel, 7, Los Angeles Times/Robert Gauthier, 29, NHLI/Dave Sandford, 27, NHLI/Harry How, 13, Sports Illustrated/David E. Klutho, 23, 25; Shutterstock: Pe3k, 24, Robert Adrian Hillman (splat), 12, 28, sabri deniz kizil, 6, 14, 22, 26, Spiroview Inc, 19, urbanbuzz, 21 (bottom left); Sports Illustrated: David E. Klutho, 15, Heinz Kluetmeier, 17, 18, Hy Peskin, 5, Manny Millan, cover (right), 21 (back)

All internet sites appearing in back matter were available and accurate when this book was sent to press.

Table of Contents

Words in **bold** are in the glossary.

The Myth of Six

The National Hockey League (NHL) has a long history. Many fans think it began in 1942 with only six teams. That's not true. The NHL began in 1917. It had several teams. These included the Senators, Bulldogs, and others.

The "Original Six" is just one hockey **myth**. Let's learn about other hockey legends.

The Original Six were six NHL teams. They included the Rangers, Bruins, Canadiens, Blackhawks, Red Wings, and Maple Leafs.

Cursed Conference Trophies

Each year, the NHL **conference** winners receive trophies. But some players don't touch it. Why? They think it could **curse** their team. How? It would keep them from winning the Stanley Cup.

The Chicago Blackhawks with the 2013 Western Conference trophy

But there is no curse. In 2020, Tampa Bay players eagerly grabbed the trophy. They did it again in 2021. What happened? The Lightning won the Stanley Cup both years.

HE THUNDER

FACT

Players began growing playoff beards in the 1980s. They do it for luck. Teams in the finals are often very hairy!

Octopus Luck?

This story is weird. But it's true! In 1950, it took eight playoff wins to win a **title**. That year, a Detroit fan threw an octopus on to the ice. Its eight arms stood for winning the championship. The Red Wings won the Stanley Cup!

Detroit fans began a new **tradition**. They snuck octopuses into the arena. Then they waited. If their team won, they tossed the creatures on to the ice. Stadium staff had to pick them up.

The Red Wings moved to a new arena in 2018. Fans wanted to honor Joe Louis Arena. They threw 35 octopuses in the final game. This custom isn't allowed anymore.

FACT

Al the Octopus now appears at the Red Wings' stadium for big playoff games.

A Golden Miracle?

A **miracle** happened in 1980. The Soviet Union's hockey team was powerful. They'd won gold medals at four straight Winter Olympics. They seemed unbeatable. The U.S. team was young and unproven. Nobody thought they'd beat the Soviets. But they did!

However, the U.S. team hadn't won gold—not yet. The "Miracle on Ice" was a **semifinal** game. The U.S. still had to beat Finland. Two days later, they did. The team won 4–2. They were Olympic champs!

FACT

In the 2002 Olympics, someone buried a Canadian dollar at center ice. The secret charm seemed to help. Canada's men's and women's hockey teams both won gold medals.

Superstar Superstitions

Some great players are **superstitious**. Wayne Gretzky is the "Great One." He holds most of the NHL's records. But he always followed a **routine**.

Before each game, Gretzky drank a Diet Coke. Then he drank ice water. Then some Gatorade. Finally, he had another Diet Coke. He thought it helped him play better.

Penguins star Sidney Crosby has several habits, too. He always sits in the same seat on the team plane. He even wears the same hat all season. In 2021, Crosby was voted the NHL's Most Superstitious Player.

One Special Cup

Most championship trophies stay in one place. But not the Stanley Cup. It's always on the go. Winning players have their names **etched** onto the Cup. Then they get to spend a day with it. The Cup has had some wild travels.

PITTSBURGH PENGUINS 2015-16

MARIO LEMIEUX RON BURKLE WILLIAM KASSLING
DAVID MOREHOUSE TRAVIS WILLIAMS JIM RUTHERFORD
JASON BOTTERILL BILL GUERIN JASON KARMANOS
MARK RECCHI MIKE SULLIVAN JACQUES MARTIN
RICK TOCCHET MIKE BALES ANDY SAUCIER
DR. DHARMESH VYAS CHRIS STEWART CURTIS BELL
PATRICK STEIDLE ANDY O'BRIEN ALEX TRINCA
DANA HEINZE TED RICHARDS JON TAGLIANETTI
JIM BRITT DAN MACKINNON RANDY SEXTON DEREK CLANCEY

15
BLUNK
SCOTTY BOWMAN
EN
THOMAS
N
Y
RY
SA BRANDON SAAD

Imagine losing the Stanley Cup! The 1924 Canadiens almost did. Some players stopped to fix a flat tire. But they made a mistake. They forgot the Cup! They left it by the road. Thankfully, it was still there when they went back.

Players have often served food in or drank from the Stanley Cup. Some have used it as a baby bathtub. Mario Lemieux once took the Cup to a pool party. But it sank to the bottom!

FACT

The New York Rangers won the Stanley Cup in 1994. They later used it to feed the winning horse of the Kentucky Derby!

Glossary

conference (KAHN-fuhr-uhns)—a group of sports teams; multiple conferences make up a league

curse (KURS)—a spell or charm that supposedly causes harm or misfortune to happen to someone

etch (ECH)—to create lettering on a hard surface by using acid

miracle (MEER-uh-kuhl)—an incredible event that isn't expected to happen

myth (MITH)—a false idea that many people believe

routine (roo-TEEN)—a regular way or pattern of doing tasks

semifinal (SEM-ee-fye-nuhl)—a game or match to determine which team advances to the championship round

superstitious (soo-puhr-STISH-uhs)—believing in following certain routines or traditions to avoid bad things from happening

title (TYE-tuhl)—an award given to the champion of a sport

tradition (truh-DISH-uhn)—a custom passed down through time

Read More

Fishman, Jon M. *Hockey's G.O.A.T.: Wayne Gretzky, Sidney Crosby, and More*. Minneapolis: Lerner, 2020.

Gish, Ashley. *Ice Hockey*. Mankato, MN: Creative Education, 2022.

Hoena, Blake. *Lake Placid Miracle: When U.S. Hockey Stunned the World*. North Mankato, MN: Capstone Press, 2019.

Internet Sites

Hockey 101
sportsnet.ca/hockey/hockey-101

Sports Illustrated Kids: Hockey
sikids.com/hockey

USA Youth Hockey
usahockey.com/comeplayyouthhockey

Index

About the Author

Elliott Smith is a former sports reporter who covered athletes in all sports from high school to the pros. He is one of the authors of the Natural Thrills series about extreme outdoor sports. In his spare time, he likes playing sports with his two children, going to the movies, and adding to his collection of Pittsburgh Steelers memorabilia.